Discarded, Date 6/94

Do You Hear

Published on the same day in Canada by Longman Canada Limited.

© Copyright 1960 by Helen Borten • Library of Congress Catalogue Card No. 60-7499 • Printed in the United States of America

ISBN: 0-200-00004-7 Reinforced Edition

Fifth Impression, 1974

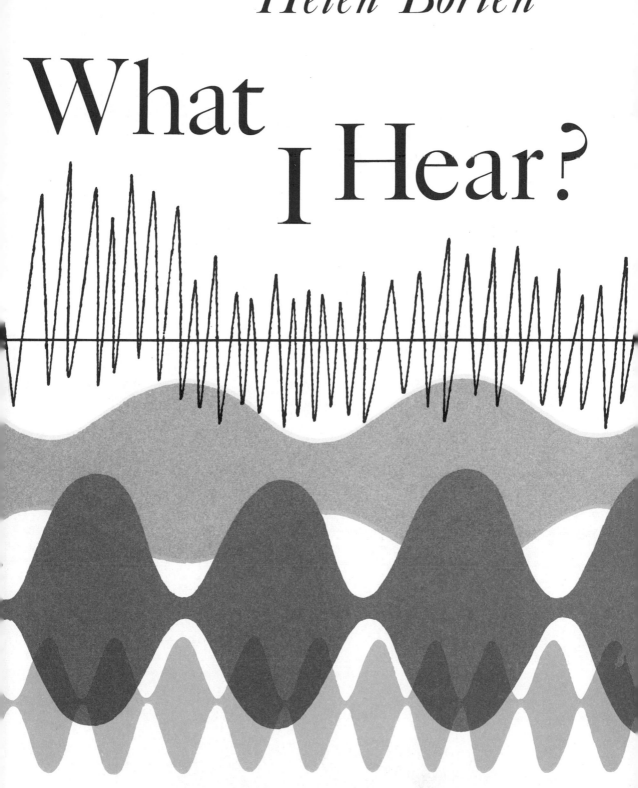

Helen Borten

What I Hear?

Abelard-Schuman
LONDON   NEW YORK
An Intext Publisher

I hear sounds everywhere around me.
Sounds can do many different things.
They can put me to sleep — like a lullaby.
Or they can wake me up — like an alarm clock.
They can take me by surprise — like a sneeze.
Or they can follow me — like an echo.

Different kinds of sounds make me feel different ways. Loud sounds can make me feel as fierce as a lion and as explosive as a firecracker. The sound of the circus fills me with excitement. I hear animals roaring, music blaring, people shouting, hands clapping, peanut shells cracking and balloons bursting.

Quiet sounds can be busy and cheerful, like clocks ticking, and crickets chirping and brooms sweeping. Or they can be as mysterious as a secret whispered in someone's ear.

Many quiet sounds make me sleepy — like rain pattering on the roof. The sound of summer makes me sleepy too. When I lie in the grass on a hot summer day, I can hear leaves rustling, flies buzzing, pigeons cooing, and I feel warm and drowsy all over.

Some sounds are so quiet you can't hear them at all.
Can you hear a daisy's petal falling?
Or a butterfly's wings beat against the air?

There are sounds as near
and warm as a kiss —
or as far off and gray as a fog horn.
Some sounds are too far away
to hear at all.
Can you hear a falling star?

A sound can go on and on like a siren or be as short
as the pop! of bubble gum. Some long sounds are
lonely like the wind wailing through the trees and a

train whistle far off in the night. Others seem to growl
with power — like an airplane engine.

The longest sound I know
is the mighty sound of the sea; it goes on and on
and *never* stops.

Short sounds
are full of energy.
They make me feel as bright
as a spark
and as bouncy as a ball.
Short sounds can be as sharp
as the crack of a whip,
as angry as the slam of a door,
or as funny
as the bark of a seal.

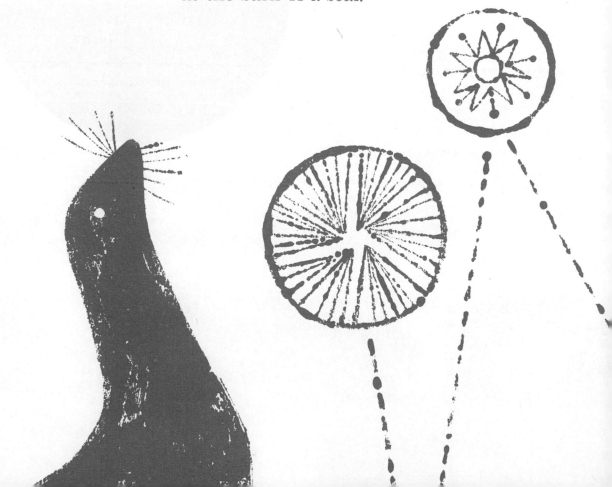

Low sounds are thick and dark — like molasses. They pull me down, down with them until I feel as squat as a bullfrog. I remember the mysterious rumble of distant thunder and the deep roar of trucks on thc highway.

High sounds are skinny, tinny sounds. They can be as cheerful as a whistling teakettle, as shrill as a scream, or as delicate as the tinkle of glass.

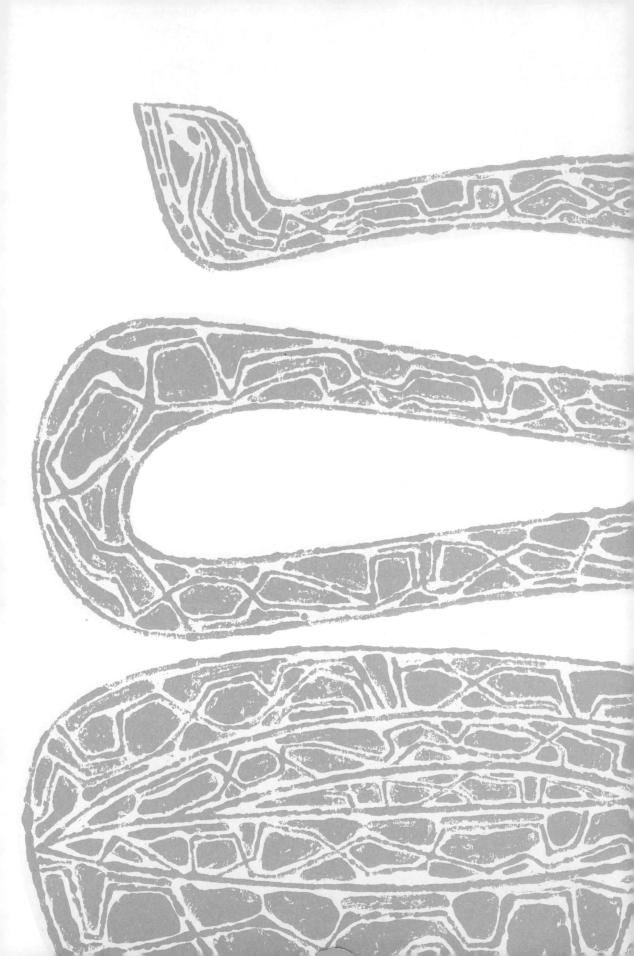

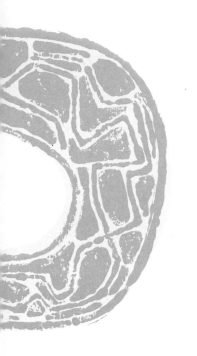

Sometimes it's not the kind of sound but what makes the sound that decides how I feel. A hiss can be frightening coming from a snake, or funny coming from a collapsing balloon. Sometimes *not* knowing what makes a sound decides how I feel. A strange rattle in the middle of the night is scary — until it turns out to be daddy, snoring.

There are sounds as harsh as my roller skates on the sidewalk or as musical as the twang of a guitar. Harsh, unmusical sounds can send shivers down my

back like the squeak of chalk on a blackboard. Or they can be as funny as the slurp of a straw in an ice cream soda.

The sound of the city is a harsh
busy sound of horns, trucks,
buses, whistles, and sirens
all mixed up together.

Musical sounds can be as sweet
as the song of the lark,
as brassy as a trumpet,
or as haunting as a church bell
in the still of the night.

The sound of Christmas is full of music and joy —
sleigh bells tinkling, carolers singing,
door bells ringing, paper and ribbons rustling.

Sometimes sounds are repeated in a definite pattern like this — RAT- tat-tat, RAT- tat-tat. That is called rhythm. With rhythm, sounds can clippety- clop like a horse, OOM- pah- pah like a big brass band, or rub-a-dub-dub like a nursery rhyme. Different rhythms make us feel different ways too. Rhythm can make my feet tap and my heart beat as fast as tom toms. Or it can be as slow and tiresome as a leaky faucet.

Music is a combination of sounds in rhythm. Did you ever hear a big orchestra play? The sounds of the

different musical instruments all blend together in a
rich symphony of sound and rhythm.

Wherever I go I hear different sounds — loud sounds and quiet sounds, long sounds and short sounds, high sounds and low sounds, harsh sounds and musical sounds. I hear squeaks and creaks and bangs and clangs; jingles and jangles and pitters and patters; tootles and tweetles and rattles and clatters; boos and moos and cock-a-doodle-doos.

The world is like a great symphony,
full of sounds to listen to and enjoy.
Do you hear what I hear?